All Bears Need Love

Tanya Valentine

ISBN-13:978-1480184817
ISBN-10:1480184810
:

For my little bear.

One summer day, Baby Brown Bear

arrived at City Zoo.

All the animals gathered to see

the new cub.

The strange new faces frightened

Baby Brown Bear.

"Come here, Baby," said Mama Polar Bear.

"I'll be your mother."

"YOU?" the other animals gasped.

"Of course," said Mama Polar Bear.

"All bears need love."

The giraffe scoffed. "But he doesn't

look like you."

"I think he's beautiful," said

Mama Polar Bear.

The elephant frowned. "But you don't know where he came from."

"What matters is that he's here now," said Mama Polar Bear.

The camel spit. "He's an outsider.

He'll never fit in."

"I'll make sure he knows he belongs

here," said Mama Polar Bear.

The hyena snickered. "Everyone

will tease him."

"I'll teach him to be proud," said

Mama Polar Bear.

The monkey screeched. "But you have

your own cubs to care for!"

"A mother's heart grows with love for

ALL her children," said Mama Polar Bear.

The anteater sniffed. "No one will believe he's yours."

"He will know," said Mama Polar Bear. "That's what's important."

The kangaroo sneered. "He's too different. This will never work!"

"Family is family, no matter the differences," said Mama Polar Bear.

The lion roared. "Will he be raised as a brown bear or a polar bear?"

"He will be the best of both," said Mama Polar Bear.

That day, the Polar Bear family grew

one Baby Brown Bear bigger.

And in the evening,

when all the animals were asleep,

only one whisper could be heard.

"Close your eyes and sleep, little one,"

Mama Polar Bear said.

"And always remember that

I am yours and you are mine

because all bears need love."

And so remained the Polar Bear family.

Until one day...

Baby Panda Bear arrived at City Zoo.

Tanya Valentine's *All Bears Need Love* was inspired by the many

unexpected questions, comments, and curiosities that accompanied

her son's adoption. She lives with her husband and children in

Atlanta, Georgia.

55236459R00020

Made in the USA
Lexington, KY
15 September 2016